SAILING MADE EASY

Told in Pictures

SAILING MADE EASY

EASY
Told in

Pictures by Rufus G. Smith

WITH SPECIAL PHOTOGRAPHS BY WALTER CIVARDI

Instructor in Photography, School of Fine and Applied Art,

Pratt Institute, Brooklyn, N. Y.

DODD, MEAD & COMPANY · NEW YORK

FOREWORD

Sailing is a great sport. Pictorially it has no peer. To know sailing is to love it and to enjoy a hobby which may be followed actively on into the years, regardless of age. Many factors are involved in sailing even a small boat skillfully, and skippers who have spent a lifetime on the water still learn something new about boats, the wind, or the water nearly every time they venture out.

Yet the rudiments of sailing are simple, much simpler than they seem to the uninitiated observer. That it often appears otherwise is because there is so much about sailing which is entirely new to the beginner. The parts of the boat, the terminology, even the few things that have a familiar counterpart ashore have a new name on the water. Getting started is the most difficult step of all.

Experience in teaching and talking of sailing to beginners has shown that pictures are invaluable aids to learning. Terms, expressions, and maneuvers can be explained in a picture or short series of pictures more clearly than in whole chapters of mere words. The primary object of this book is to define, describe, and teach the fundamentals of sailing in a graphic manner, easily remembered and readily referred to.

Obtaining the pictures was not easy; for completing the work meant many takes and retakes, getting our models and ourselves on the job day after day, and when all the principals were ready to go, there was still the question of sufficient wind and proper light for good pictures.

In that connection I wish to express my gratitude to my colleague, Walter Civardi, whose expert knowledge of photography was matched only by his patience and splendid spirit of co-operation without which this book could never have been done.

Thanks are also due Miss Jean Clinton and Mr. Jack Seaver who spent many long hours being photographed and waiting for the wind during most of a summer.

The Cape Cod Senior Knockabout illustrated in most of the pictures was very kindly loaned for the purpose by the Cape Cod Shipbuilding Corporation.

To Morris Rosenfeld, Photographic Illustrator, I am especially indebted. Without his copious files of thousands of extraordinary photographs of all kinds of sailing craft, diversification in the number and character of boats and situations illustrated would not have been possible. Among the other photographers whose work contributed greatly is Chester Rogers of Baytown, Texas, who took special photographs for the revised edition.

LaPorte, Texas   RUFUS G. SMITH

CONTENTS

INTRODUCTION

From time to time we have attempted to explain something about sailing to various types of beginners. Some of these had never been near the water, others had seen boats sailing, and still others claimed a little experience as passengers on boats being handled by experienced skippers. To all of them, sailing was still pretty much a mystery. Even those who had actually sailed remembered the experience mainly as a complicated series of maneuvers interspersed with commands and comments in a lingo which was utterly strange and bewildering. The sails had moved from side to side every time the boat turned, sometimes slowly and easily, sometimes with a wallop and bang which all but swept the occupants out of the boat. One moment the boat would be leaning over at an unearthly angle with spray flying on all sides, and a few moments later without much apparent slackening of the wind, they would be sailing serenely along without a drop of water on deck. What, why, how come? Without the aid of some step by step explanation it was pretty hard to really understand what was happening or might be coming next.

On other occasions we have witnessed the progress of people attempting to learn to sail through the pages of a book. There the going is usually difficult because there are so many nautical terms which can only be defined and explained with the use of equally baffling expressions. Unless there is a boat at hand, in which each step can be tried out as it is discussed in the book, the would-be-sailor soon becomes bogged down in a maze of terminology and maneuvers exceedingly difficult to visualize.

In this book, through the use of pictures, we attempt to avoid such pitfalls. Every term, every maneuver is illustrated as simply as possible and in logical sequence. However, nobody ever learned to sail without sailing; books can help and pictures can help a great deal, but you will have to supplement them with some actual experience before all the pieces really fit together.

Don't try to learn everything at once. Do check through and try out the maneuvers in your boat. If you don't comprehend everything in the pictures and captions the first time you go through the book, with more experience and greater understanding the minor points will become increasingly clear. Keep going through the book as you continue to sail, it will help to clarify and impress the things you will be learning by experience in your boat.

Everything you will eventually want to know is not told in this book, and some of the peculiarities of your own boat obviously are not covered. But we have tried to cover the necessary rudiments which apply to all boats, and enough more to whet the appetite for more information and more enjoyment.

PARTS OF THE BOAT

AND THEIR PURPOSES

Learn the proper seagoing terms for the various parts of your boat. Many of them will be entirely new to you, while other more familiar objects have a different name than ashore.

Mast — The vertical spar on which the sails are hoisted.

Boom — The horizontal spar to which the lower edge of the mainsail is fastened.

Boomcrotch—A removable support for the boom, for use when the sail is not set.

Main Shrouds — Pieces of wire fastened to or around the mast and extending down to the sides of the boat. Note: Only the wires at the *side* of the mast are properly termed shrouds.

Jib stay—A wire leading to the deck ahead of the mast to give it forward support and on which the jib is set. Note: Wires leading down *ahead* and *behind* the mast are always called stays.

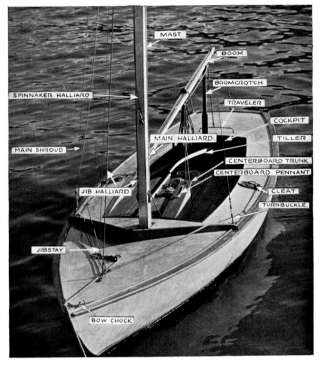

Turnbuckle — A metal screw contrivance for keeping the proper tension on shrouds and stays. The turnbuckle identified above is on the main shroud.

Jib Halliard, Main Halliard, Spinnaker Halliard — Lines running up the mast and down again for setting (pulling up) the jib, mainsail and spinnaker respectively. Halliards should never be called ropes.

Cleat — A piece of metal or wood with two horns around which halliards or other lines are fastened.

Centerboard Trunk — A housing around the centerboard's "up" position.

Centerboard Pennant — A rope or wire passing through the top of the trunk and used for raising and lowering the centerboard.

Tiller — The tiller is connected to the rudder post and is used for steering the boat.

Cockpit — The open portion of the boat which is not decked over.

Traveler — or *Deck Horse* — An athwartship rod enabling the mainsheet blocks (pullies), to follow the boom from one side of the boat to the other.

Bow Chock — An elliptical or circular shape, usually of metal, cut away at the top and into which the mooring line, anchor line or towline is dropped to keep it pulling directly from the bow.

THE HULL

Topsides — The sides of the boat, above the level at which it floats.

Boot-top — The area at and near the waterline when painted a distinctive color.

Bottom — The area below the level at which the boat floats.

Keel — The backbone of a boat to which other structural parts are fastened. Also, in some small boats, a ballasted fin at the bottom which contributes to stability.

Deadwood — The solid timbering just ahead of the rudder.

Rudder — A flat piece which is swung back and forth. Its action turns the boat.

THE SAILS, SPARS AND RIGGING

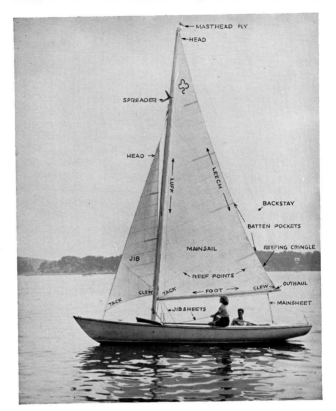

Foot—The lower edge of a sail.

Luff—The forward edge of a sail.

Leech—The after edge of a sail.

Tack — The corner of a sail between the foot and the luff.

Clew — The corner of a sail between the foot and the leech.

Head—The top corner of a sail.

Mainsail — The sail set on the after side of the mainmast.

Jib — A sail set forward of the mast.

Mainsheet — A line used to control the angle at which the mainsail is set. Call it a sheet not a rope. It usually works through blocks on the deck and boom.

Jib Sheets — The lines used to control the jib. They are fastened to the sail at the clew.

Batten Pockets — Long thin pockets in the sail at right angles to the leech into which strips of wood or plastic are placed to keep the sail from flapping and help hold its proper shape.

Reef Points — A row of reinforced holes in the sail parallel to its foot and sometimes containing short lengths of line for reefing the sail.

Reefing Cringle — A large reinforced eye sewed into the sail, which is lashed to the boom when the sail is reefed. It must then bear the strain ordinarily borne by the cringle in the clew.

Outhaul — A device which slides on a track at the end of the boom and to which the clew of the sail is fastened.

Backstay — A wire leading from the masthead or some point well above deck to the after part of the boat to give support to the mast.

Masthead Fly — A metal or fabric streamer which indicates the direction of the wind.

Spreaders — Wood or metal arms at right angles to the mast, over the ends of which the shrouds are passed to provide additional support.

These extend across the full width of the boat:

Bow — The forward part of the boat.

Amidships — The middle of the boat.

Stern — The extreme after end of the boat.

Forward — Toward the bow.

Aft — Toward the stern.

Starboard — The right side of the boat, looking forward.

Port — The left side of the boat, looking forward. Keep port and starboard straight by remembering, "Jack left port."

Quarter — The sides of the boat aft of amidships.

Aloft — Above the heads of people standing on deck.

Windward — The side of the boat and general direction *from* which the wind is blowing.

Leeward — The side of the boat and general direction *toward* which the wind is blowing.

Abeam — At right angles to the line of the keel.

Stem — The foremost timber of the boat.

THE DIRECTION OF THE WIND

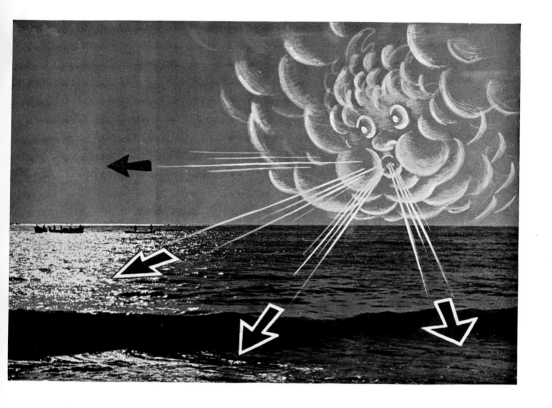

Arrows like these are used on the following pictures to indicate the direction from which the wind is blowing in each photograph. Whether it is North, South, East, or West is of no significance here. But its relative direction is of constant importance to the angle to the centerline of our boat at which our sails are set, the points on the opposite shore toward which we can sail, and many other factors. The experienced sailor almost instinctively keeps a constant check on the wind direction. As he approaches the water, or comes on deck if already aboard, he notices it; and as he sails or otherwise moves about the water he is on the alert for signs of major and even minor changes in the wind.

Make things shipshape as soon as you get aboard. Sheets and halliards should be in their proper places and neatly coiled to run out freely when needed. Pump, anchor line, spare gear, etc., should be properly stowed. Make sure your halliards are clear *aloft* before fastening them to the heads of the sails. This one is fouled around a spreader. Sail slides may be run onto either mast or boom

first. Keep all the sail up out of the bottom of the boat where it might become wet and dirty. The halliard is already fastened to the head of the sail. Follow the foot of the sail from the tack out to the clew to make sure there are no twists in it. Then run the slides on the boom, still keeping the sail out of the bottom of the boat. Pull the foot of the sail out, hand-tight only. With a new sail par-

FOR GETTING UNDER WAY

ticularly, do not put all your strength on it or you will soon have the foot pulled out beyond the end of the boom and the sail out of shape, or "nigger-heeled." As it stretches with use, pull out the outhaul to take up the slack. Don't forget the battens — top and bottom are usually the shortest. Be sure to fasten the tie lines through the holes in the battens as well as both the holes in the sail. Note

that the sail is hung over the boom, not lying on the floor of the cockpit. Hook the jib on the jibstay. Make sure the head (the narrowest corner) is at the top. Hoist the mainsail first (or whatever sail is farthest aft on your boat), with the bow of the boat heading directly into the wind. If you hoist the jib first the wind will catch it, pull bow away from the wind, making it difficult to set mainsail.

Everyone aboard tails onto the main halliard of the big Class J racer "Yankee" to raise the heavy mainsail quickly. Once you start to raise a sail, get it up as rapidly as possible to keep it from fouling spreaders, backstays, and other gear and to get it clear of the deck before the wind takes hold and starts to move the boat.

A *Gaff Headed Rig*. The mainsail is four-sided instead of three-sided as in the more common Marconi rig. Such sails are usually laced onto the boom and gaff (the extra spar aloft) with lacing lines which pass round and round the spars and through grommets along the foot and peak of the sail. Two halliards are used in raising the mainsail, the peak halliard which attaches near the center of the gaff, and the throat halliard at its inner end which keeps the luff of the sail tight. Notice that the foot of the jib carries a boom.

MAKING SAIL

Loosen the mainsheet as the sail goes up and allow it to run freely and the sail to spill the wind.

"Sway" on the halliard to get the sail up tight. The skipper holds a turn under the cleat as the crew pulls *out* and then quickly *in* and *down*. — But again, don't stretch a new sail too tight.

CONTINUED

Hoist the jib after mainsail is set and swinging freely. Don't sway on it so much that you pull the mast forward.

Hook in the jib sheets — being careful to avoid twists in the lines.
The boat is now ready to "get under way" (to start sailing).

Sailing before the wind. The boat is parallel or nearly parallel to the direction the wind. The boom and sails are right angles to the wind — Also known "sailing down wind" — and "running

A piece of ribbon tied to the shrouds makes an excellent "telltale" to show the exact direction of the wind.

Sailing on a broad reach. The boat sailing across the wind, with wind directly abeam, or aft of abeam.

The relative direction of the wind to your course, or the direction in which you wish to sail, is very important to the angle at which the sails are carried or "trimmed." "Running," "Reaching," and "Close-Hauled" are the principal "points" of sailing, and each calls for the sails to be set at a different angle.

Sailing on a close reach. The boat is still sailing across the wind but with the wind coming from slightly forward of abeam. The sails are more nearly parallel to the center line of the boat.

Sailing close-hauled. The boat is sailing at an angle of only about 45 degrees from the direction of the wind — as close as she can go and still keep moving effectively. Sails are nearly parallel to the center line of the boat. Also known as sailing "on the wind."

"Trimming" sheets means pulling in the sheets and thus, too, the sails. Also termed "flattening" sheets. Remember that the "sheets" are the lines or ropes used to control the sails, not the sails themselves.

"Slacking" sheets means letting out the sheets and thus, too, the sails. Also termed "cracking" sheets and "easing" sheets. Notice how the boat has straightened up as the sheets are slacked off.

TRIMMING AND

SLACKING SHEETS

Sails are shifted to the exact positions required by the various points of sailing by "trimming" and "slacking."

Trimming sheets on a Cup Defender means work for all hands, even though powerful winches multiply the pull of human arms many times. Here are two groups flattening down "Ranger's" headsail sheets.

The bow of the boat moves in a direction opposite to that in which the tiller is moved. Think of the tiller as "pushing" the stern of the boat around — Or "pulling" the stern around. (Dotted lines show the boat's wake — i.e. the direction from which the boat has come.)

THE ACTION OF THE TILLER

AND RUDDER

In a fast moving boat only a slight movement of the tiller is required to change her course.

Putting the wheel over. Practically all wheels swing the bow in the direction the wheel is turned. — Note how the mainsheet is snubbed around the cleat as it is hauled in.

A *few pages back we left the boa* *with sails set — all ready to get un* *der way.*

Next, drop the centerboard half way down as a precautionary measure, even though in reaching and running you may not need its lateral resistance. Using the centerboard helps the boat respond to her rudder.

The crew unfastens the mooring line (or pulls up the anchor) and holds line in her hand. Skipper grasps tiller and mainsheet which is *not* trimmed in tight.

Crew (still holding mooring line) "backs" the jib by holding it out against the wind. Skipper pulls tiller to same side of boat to help the bow fall off away from the wind.

As the wind acting on the jib begins to push the bow off, crew casts off mooring line and skipper trims his mainsheet so the mainsail catches the wind and boat begins to move ahead.

The boat is under way (moving ahead). Crew releases jib and comes into cockpit to trim it on the proper side — through the leeward leads* and with the leeward sheets — never ahead of the mast with windward sheets (except when "backing" the jib). Jib should be trimmed to approximately same angle as mainsail.

* *Leads* — Metal eyes fastened to the deck through which the jib sheets are led in order to equalize the tension on the foot and leech of the jib.

The jib of a Corinthian Class boat is "backed" by holding it out against the wind in order to swing the boat quickly and sharply in getting away from a pier. Trimming the sheets on the windward or "wrong" side is a less effective means of backing the jib.

Don't tie the mainsheet down hard on the cleat on a small centerboard boat. A half-turn or, at most, a full turn is sufficient to hold the strain. By holding the end in his hand the skipper can slack off quickly in case a hard puff of wind strikes the sail.

Making sail and preparations for getting under way on a large yawl. The aftermost sail, the mizzen, has been set first and is sheeted in flat to keep the boat heading up into the wind. Next the mainsail has been set, and here the crew is ready to hoist the forestaysail and jib all ready to go, up forward.

31

REACHING . . .

As the wind fills the sails on casting off from mooring or dock, the boat gathers headway (moves faster and faster) for several seconds. The skipper and crew watch telltales and other signs to check whether or not the sails are "trimmed" properly, i.e. set at the proper angle to the wind. The boat is now on a reach, the simplest "point" of sailing — with the wind abeam (Page 22).

On a reach or a run a straight course may be sailed by heading for a point on the shore in line with wherever you desire to go (like the high trees here). Weight of skipper and crew may be placed to off-set the force of the wind on the sails and keep the boat as nearly vertical as possible. Practice steering to accustom yourself to the response of the boat to her helm.

OR SAILING

ACROSS THE WIND

When you head more directly into the wind or the wind shifts to come from farther ahead, the sails will luff, i.e. the wind will strike them on the lee side near the luff. They will shake and flutter. You must trim them flatter or change your course to head farther off the wind.

When you head farther off the wind or the wind comes from farther aft, you will have to slack off the sheets. Until you gain experience in trimming your sails from the wind direction as shown by the masthead fly or telltales, the best way will be to slack off the sheet to the point at which the sail begins to luff—then trim it in a little so that the whole sail is just full.

As long as the wind remains in the same direction you can sail on and on without changing the position or "trim" of the sails. The full-rigged ship "Seven Seas" and ocean-racing schooners like "Mistress" sometimes sail for days at a time in parts of the oceans where winds are steady, hardly touching a sheet or a halliard.

When on a reach, if you want to return to or near your starting point you must turn by tacking (pages 36 & 37) or jibing (page 50).

Still on a reach, the skipper gives th[
command, "Stand by to tack," meaning
get ready to tack. The crew looks t[
windward and astern to make certai[
that they are clear of other boats an[
prepares to let go the jib sheets.

With the command "Hard-a-lee," th[
skipper puts the tiller hard over to th[
leeward side, which swings the bow int[
the wind. The jib sheets are cast off an[
overhauled.* The mainsheet need no[
be changed although it must not b[
cleated down hard.

* *Overhauled* — Pulled out through thei[
leads and blocks.

he easiest way to turn is to "tack" or
"come about," one of the most impor-
nt maneuvers in sailing. Turn your
ow into the wind, i.e., in the direc-
on from which the wind is coming,
nd on around so that the wind comes
ver the opposite side of the boat.

he boat straightens up and the sails
utter as the bow continues to swing
round.

As the wind strikes the sails on the opposite side, the tiller is straightened out
and the jib sheets trimmed under the
boom again. The boat regains headway,
now on a starboard reach and returning
in the general direction whence she has
come. Trim is adjusted as it was on the
port reach but with everything on the
opposite side.

A big, heavy boat, in tacking, has sufficient momentum to carry for several boat lengths right into the eye of the wind. Here "Endeavour II," in the foreground, has just tacked along the course indicated by the dotted line from almost the same position here occupied by "Ranger." She has traveled between three and four lengths dead to windward.

BEATING TO WINDWARD

(Known also as "turning to windward")

In reaching you have observed that the flatter you trim your sails the more closely into the wind your boat will sail and, unless the water is quite rough, the faster she will go.

Beating to windward is in reality reaching as close to the wind as the boat can head and still maintain good speed through the water.

BEATING TO

WINDWARD

Drop the centerboard all the way down to provide maximum "lateral resistance" and counteract the tendency for the boat to slide sidewise or "make leeway" which develops as the sails are trimmed in flat.

Trim your sails in as flat as possible and move the tiller so that the boat gradually heads up more directly into the wind. To counteract the greater tendency to heel over, skipper and crew both sit on the windward side. There is a certain optimum point at which the boat heads high into the wind and still maintains good speed through the water. This is from 40 degrees to 60 degrees away from the wind depending on the boat, the strength of the wind, the character of the sea, and many other factors.

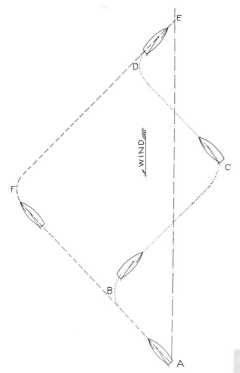

By sailing back and forth at about 45 degrees from the wind, you eventually work out dead to windward (A to E). Each jog (AB, BC, etc.,) is called a "tack" or a "board." From A to E can be made in two long tacks (AFE) or several short tacks (ABCDE).

Finding the optimum point and keeping your boat moving to windward at its best, is one of the most difficult operations in sailing. Different boats vary so much in this respect that only practice and experiment can teach you all the tricks of your own boat.

If you trim still flatter you can point higher into the wind but your boat will lose speed through the water. Note how she has straightened up in this picture. This is sometimes known as "pinching" or "starving" the boat. By heading more directly into the wind there is less distance between you and your objective, but your speed is reduced disproportionately. Conversely, if you sail too far off the wind ("too full") your boat will make faster speed through the water but will have more distance to cover.

TACKING

Tacking when beating to windward is essentially the same maneuver as when reaching (Pages 36, 37, 38).

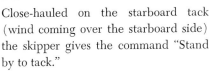

Close-hauled on the starboard tack (wind coming over the starboard side) the skipper gives the command "Stand by to tack."

"Hard-a-Lee" is the command given as the skipper puts the tiller over and the crew lets go the jib sheets and trims the jib on the other side. Don't swing the boat too sharply, yet not so slowly that you lose all headway.

As the sails fill on the other tack and the boat regains headway the skipper slacks the mainsheet a bit to help the boat gain speed through the water. In a few minutes he will trim in flatter and head the boat up to the optimum point. Note that in this picture the boat is at about 90 degrees to its course in the picture above. In both cases they are about 45 degrees from the wind.

Stars beating to windward in a hard breeze. Note that the boat on the port tack is sailing a course approximately at right angles to that of the boats on the star-board tack.

In beating to windward the object is to attain the optimum combination of speed through the water and a close angle to the wind.

To accomplish this:

 A. Keep the weight of skipper and crew as far up to windward as convenient in order to keep the boat standing up straight on her best sailing lines.

 B. Watch the luffs of jib and mainsail to guard against pointing too high in the wind — above the optimum point.

 C. At the same time watch the telltales or masthead pennant to be sure you do not fall too far off the wind — below the optimum point.

 D. Experiment a bit with slight changes in the trim of the sheets. Two or three inches one way or another often make quite a difference in the speed of the boat through the water. If there is a lot of strain on the tiller — ease off the mainsheet a bit — you are trimmed too flat. In a strong breeze it may even be best to let the mainsail luff a bit.

 E. As you gain in experience it will become easier to tell whether or not your boat is going to windward at her best. A glance at the telltales will show whether or not you are sailing at the best angle to the wind. The ears can tell whether or not the sound and cadence of the bow pushing into the waves are correct. And eventually all the senses will combine to tell you whether or not the "feel" of the boat is right.

TRIMMING THE

SAILS PROPERLY

Only experience can teach you just how best to trim your sails. But, look out for:

A mainsail trimmed too flat — Note how the leech is practically a straight line from masthead to end of boom. There is no flow to the sail. The jib is trimmed correctly.

A mainsail too far off for windward work. — There is flow to the sail here — but the boat could not possibly hold up to the optimum point without carrying a big luff in the sail. The jib is trimmed correctly.

The mainsail is trimmed properly but the jib is too flat for the light wind in this picture. The jib is "flat as a board."

The jib is slacked off too much in this picture. Its whole forward edge is luffing. The mainsail is trimmed correctly for the light breeze, though with more wind it could be flatter.

RUNNING . . . OR SAILING

Running before the wind is essentially the simplest and often the pleasantest "point" of sailing. But beginners should be careful to avoid an unintentional jibe which may involve a peck of trouble.

On a broad reach the wind flows off the leech of the mainsail as indicated by the arrows. Thus, the force on the after edge (leech) is intensified, tending to pull the stern to leeward. This must be offset by the rudder.

But if you head farther off the wind, suddenly a point is reached where the strain on the tiller eases up and the boat is easier to steer. She straightens up, does not heel at all, in fact. She is running before the wind with part of the air flowing around the mast as indicated by the arrows.

BEFORE THE WIND

These two pictures were taken only a few minutes apart. With the wind dead aft the boom may be on either side of the boat. When dead before the wind, be very careful not to head so far off that the wind is coming from your lee quarter, otherwise you may jibe (Page 50 and 51) unintentionally. To guard against this, watch the masthead fly and keep the wind dead aft or a bit on the windward quarter. Jibe properly as soon as the wind works around the least bit to the same side of the boat on which the boom is being carried.

The centerboard may be pulled all the way up as its lateral resistance is no longer needed (although in a hard breeze some board reduces the tendency to roll). The sail is slacked off to about 90 degrees from the wind. The mainsail blankets (cuts off) most of the wind from the jib but the latter may be held out by hand, or on a whisker pole, or a spinnaker may be set.

\ whisker pole winging out the jib of a Star before the wind.

Atlantic and Victory class boats rounding a mark and going from a beat to windward to a run. A-35 is already hoisting her spinnaker.

A cutter running before the wind with a squaresail set and over it a raffee. These sails are usually carried only by yachts making long passages down the "Trades" where a following wind holds steadily for thousands of miles. The hazards of jibing are eliminated and steering is much easier than with the mainsail and other fore and aft rig sails. The two holes in the squaresail are intended to release part of the air in the sail and thus develop more efficient flow and more pulling power.

A PROPER JIBE

Jibing is the act of turning the stern of the boat into and through the direction from which the wind is coming and at the same time swinging the boom or letting the wind swing it to the opposite side. Jibing is a perfectly legitimate maneuver when properly performed. But an improper or unintentional jibe can cause trouble.

The crew drops the centerboard a bit to steady the boat when the boom goes over. The skipper trims in the mainsheet, preparatory to the wind's pushing the mainsail over and to keep the boom from lifting up as it goes across.

The mainsheet is then slacked off to let the boom out at 90 degrees to the wind again.

Watch your heads! As the main boom approaches the center of the boat the tiller is swung sharply over. The stern (not the bow as in tacking) swings into the wind and the sail goes over with a bang. Note the leech of the sail which has not yet filled with wind. The mainsheet is allowed to run to absorb the shock of the boom and sail crashing over.

AN IMPROPER JIBE

Don't Do This!!

Grabbing the boom and pulling it across without trimming the sheet, or allowing the wind to throw it across without trimming will lead to . . .

the wind lifting up the boom and crashing it against the backstay or hooking the upper part of the sail around a spreader, called "goosewinging" the sail.

Even if the boom gets all the way over without tangling up, it will have so much force behind it that it will force the bow way up into the wind.

IN JIBING—

Watch Your Step!

These Sound Interclubs running befor
a hard northwester had to jibe when th
wind shifted a bit. Most of them pe:
formed the maneuver successfully . .

But — This mainsail "goosewinged'
around a port spreader, and broke it of
as the lower half of the sail jibed over
The unsupported mast bowed . . .

and broke about ten feet above deck.

When running before the wind it is a simple matter to swing back without jibing . . .

to a reach or . . .

on the wind.

THE PROPER WAY

Always come up to the mooring with the bow of your boat heading directly into the wind and sheets loose. Round up far enough away so that your headway will just carry you to the mooring. This distance will depend on many factors, including momentum, strength of the wind, character of the sea. In this picture with a light breeze and smooth water, the boat will carry its headway for several boat lengths. Heavy keel boats would carry more than twice as many lengths — light, flat bottomed craft only half as many.

The crew picks up the buoy just as the boat comes to a stop with the bow pointing directly into the wind. The skipper looks aloft to make sure the boat remains headed directly into the wind. The mainsheet is allowed to run freely.

The crew quickly fastens the mooring line while the skipper uncleats the jib halliard.

TO PICK UP

THE MOORING

The jib is lowered away as soon as possible to keep it from filling with wind and pulling the bow off which tends to make the mainsail fill also.

Leave the jib on deck and lower the mainsail as soon as you can get the boom crotch in position.

Don't forget to remove the battens from the mainsail before putting the sail in the sailbag. Long battens break very easily. Coil up sheets, halliards, etc. and make everything shipshape before leaving the boat.

"DON'TS" IN PICKING UP THE MOORING

Never, never, pick up a mooring while sailing down wind. Always swing up into the wind from the leeward side of a mooring.

Don't try to hold onto the buoy if your headway carries you beyond it. Let it go and round up again farther to leeward. If you try to hold it — the sails will fill and you will have great difficulty in lowering them.

The ocean racing yawl, "Dorade," rounding up to an anchorage. Her forestaysail is already on deck and her mainsail is being lowered. Always lower the sail farthest forward first and work aft, in order.

Head up into the wind whenever possible as in coming up to the mooring, far enough away so that you lose headway just as your bow reaches the dock. Have a line ready to make fast whether or not there is a helping hand on the dock.

The crew throws the line as soon as she is sure she is within range. The boat is headed toward the corner so that it can easily be swung clear if it still has considerable headway and might be damaged in coming in too fast.

A proper landing brings the boat in just close enough for the bow to be stopped without ever striking the dock.

Shoot by the corner and alongside or do it all over again rather than ram head-on into the dock if you are moving a bit too fast.

When the wind is blowing straight toward the only available landing place a good landing is difficult but still possible.

Slack your sheets to spill as much wind as possible and thereby cut your speed. As you get in close swing into the wind as much as possible. Putting the rudder hard over will permit it to act as a brake.

Once the boat loses headway she can be held alongside easily even though the sails are partly full.

Never sail in head-on with all sails pulling, regardless of the direction of the wind. There is never any excuse for this.

Heading up directly into the wind is the most important part of any maneuver connected with stopping the boat, whether picking up a mooring, coming alongside a dock or another boat, or on any other occasion.

In getting away from a dock with the wind blowing directly toward it, slack the jib and push the bow straight out. Then have someone push ahead on the end of the main boom. This pushes the bow further out and at the same time provides headway. The sails are then trimmed and the boat is under way again.

RULES OF THE ROAD

A few simple Rules of the Road determine which boat has right of way when two or more boats approach each other. The purpose of these rules is to prevent collision and they apply whether the boats are racing or not. In sailing races there are a great many other rules covering the fine points but these Rules of the Road are the fundamentals.

When the boats are sailing with booms on opposite sides, the boat with her boom to port (on starboard tack) has right of way. Here the little Comet with her boom to port is on starboard tack and has right of way over our Senior Knockabout.

When two boats are sailing converging courses with booms on the same side, the boat to leeward has right of way. Here our Senior Knockabout, to windward, must keep clear of the Comet. A boat being overtaken by another on the same course has right of way over the boat overtaking. Here the Senior Knockabout in passing the Comet has kept clear and has politely passed to leeward.

64

A boat under sail has right of way over any vessel under power and it is "good boating manners" for the motorboat to pass astern of the sailboat. But . . .

if a big steamer comes along don't go any closer than this Twelve-Metre did.

The little Snipe, on starboard tack in the foreground, has right of way over the big Twelve-Metres coming up across her bow on port tack, but many a sailor has had reason to recall the ditty:

"Here lies the body of Edward Day,

    Who died defending his right of way.

        He was right, dead right, as he sped along,

            But he's just as dead as if he'd been wrong.'

When two boats approach each other on opposite tacks, the boat on port tack (the "burdened vessel") must keep clear. Here the little Teal, No. 7, on starboard tack has right of way and the Corinthian, No. 25, tacks to keep clear. Or . . .

In the same situation, with Teal No. 7 still having right of way, Corinthian 25 bears off to pass astern.

SAILING IN A HARD BREEZE

There is considerable difference in the way various boats handle in a hard breeze. Experiment with changes in trim on your boat to learn the best combinations.

It is always helpful to keep the weight of skipper and crew as far up to windward as possible.

It may be necessary to carry a big luff in your mainsail to keep the boat on her feet. Most boats sail best in a strong breeze by trimming the jib quite flat and permitting the mainsail to luff considerably. Note that the mainsheet is not cleated down hard.

In righting a capsized boat, first cast off the halliards and get the sails down. Then lift up on the mast and get the boat in alongside a dock or another boat and pump or bail it dry. It may require fast work at first to take water out of the boat faster than it comes in through the open top of the centerboard trunk.

A knockdown puff in a hard breeze catches a Star boat without head-way and with her jib "backed" to windward, but letting go the jib and main sheets will bring her up again in a hurry.

SAILING IN VERY

LIGHT AIRS

In slacking sheets in light airs it is sometimes necessary to overhaul them, that is, to pull them out through their blocks and leads by hand.

Stand against the boom to hold it well out when running before a very light breeze. The cut of some sails tends to make the boom swing inboard.

Keep the weight of skipper and crew to leeward when beating to windward in light airs to give a little draft to the sails. Don't trim the sails too flat and sail farther off the wind than you ordinarily do.

Snipes beating to windward in light air. Note that skippers and crews are keeping their weight to leeward.

Exactly when to reef or otherwise shorten sail depends largely upon the characteristics of the boat, as some boats will carry full sail in a hard breeze a lot better than others. However, after you have left your dock or mooring, it is a lot easier to shake out a reef than to tie one in . . . so play safe. And remember that out on the open Bay, Lake or Sound, the wind blows a lot harder than in the protected anchorages along their edges.

Tie the reefing cringle down into the gooseneck* with several turns of stout line. The foot of the sail is fastened and pulled out on the boom just as if full sail was to be carried. Then . . .

Tie a length of line through the reefing cringle in the leech and tie the line through the outhaul and stretch the sail out tight along the line of reef points. Then . . .

Tie the cringle down tight with several turns of line extending around the boom. Then . . .

* *Gooseneck* — The hinge-like fitting connecting the boom to the mast and into which the clew of the mainsail is fastened.

Gather in the sail between the reefing eyes and the foot rope as compactly as possible and run a continuous line through all the eyes and the space between the foot rope and the boom (not under the whole boom) tying a half hitch at each reef point.

After the line has been rove and hitched through all the reefing eyes, work in on it again to take up all slack. Finish off by tying it into the gooseneck.

The boat is handled with a reef just as with full sail.

A little schooner in a hard breeze. Two-masted boats can shorten sail by lowering some sails entirely or reefing. This one has done both — jib and foresail have been taken in and the mainsail has been reefed. The forestaysail is kept up to keep the rig balanced.

HANDLING THE SPINNAKER

A spinnaker may be carried by any boat large enough to accommodate the three or more people usually necessary to handle the boat and set the spinnaker. Spinnakers are usually set in stops (tied with light, easily broken pieces of cord or thread), and the sail broken out of the stops after it has been hoisted. A clean, reasonably level stretch should be utilized for stopping the sail. The deck of the boat carrying the spinnaker is usually sufficient.

STOPPING THE
SPINNAKER

Tie the head of the sail down with a short length of line.

Pull the leeches* and all the loose canvas away from the head so that it is not bunched up.

With the leeches* held together, fold or roll the canvas up to them, taking care to keep the leeches always on the outside. Fold or roll the whole length of the sail as tightly as possible before tying any of it. Pull away from the lashing at the head constantly.

---

* *Leeches* — A spinnaker has two leeches instead of a luff and a leech like a sail set on a mast or stay.

Tie tightly around the sail with a single length of light cotton sewing thread or "rotten" string. The top stop will be the most difficult to break out so keep it at least three feet below the head of the sail.

Tie a stop around the spinnaker at intervals of every three feet, pulling away from the head at all times and keeping the sail folded or rolled as tightly as possible. One person rolls while the other ties. As you work down, the number of turns of thread or "rotten" string can be gradually increased until at the foot, four or five turns can be used. The completely stopped spinnaker is put in the sail bag and put aboard the boat.

The spinnaker is carried when running before the wind or on a broad reach. The pole is always set on the side opposite the main boom.

First rig the after and forward guys on the outer end of the spinnaker pole. The outer ends of the guys should be provided with snap shackles for rapid handling. Notice the after guy leads outside main shroud. The forward guy is made fast here to mooring cleat.

Hoist the spinnaker and fasten it to the end of the pole which is still lying on deck. On larger boats the pole is rigged and swung out with the aid of a spinnaker pole lift before the sail is fastened to the end. Lead the spinnaker sheet from the lee side around forward of the jibstay and fasten it to the clew (free corner) of the spinnaker.

The spinnaker pole is put in place on the mast and by means of the guys swung into approximately the proper position for the angle of the wind.

THE SPINNAKER
SETTING
AND BREAKING OUT

With the spinnaker completely broken out and arching out ahead, the jib is lowered away and left on deck.

By adjusting the trim of the guys and the sheet, the spinnaker can be set at its most efficient angle, keeping the pole at about 90 degrees to the direction of the wind. In light to moderate breezes with the wind well aft, the forward guy may seem superfluous, but in a hard breeze it prevents the end of the pole from lifting up.

The spinnaker is now ready to be broken out, so give a sharp pull on the sheet to break the lower stops. The wind should do the rest. Adjust after guy, forward guy, and sheet so that the sail is full and pulling. In light airs the spinnaker may be set "flying", without stopping it.

The spinnaker can be carried on a broad reach and with the wind on around to almost abeam by slacking the pole forward almost to the jibstay. Experiment with varying amounts of trim on the forward guy and lead the sheet well aft for best results.

One of the famous International Class racing on Long Island Sound with a perfectly set spinnaker. Note that both corners of the sail are kept at the same height above the deck level.

TAKING IN THE

SPINNAKER

First slack off on the after guy so the pole swings forward and the spinnaker is blanketed under the lee of the mainsail. Then remove the pole from the mast, and the sail from the end of the pole.

Lower away on the halliard and as the sail comes down gather it under the main boom and into the cockpit. *Don't* let the sail or the pole get in the water.

Spinnaker guys and pole are unrigged and brought into the cockpit and the halliard is snapped off the sail. Note the loose end of the halliard fouled around the port shroud. It should be cleared immediately.

Blanketing a spinnaker, preparatory lowering by allowing it to swing into the lee of the mainsail. The larger the boat and the spinnaker, the more important is the smooth handling of this maneuver.

Stretch your sails out to dry whenever they are wet. Never, never leave a wet or damp sail packed up in a sailbag or rolled up in a wad any longer than necessary to get them ashore. Sails dry quickly in the sun but don't leave them in it any longer than necessary as the sun rapidly bleaches out the creamy color of new sails. In damp weather spread wet sails out in a dry attic or locker room to permit the air to get at all parts of them.

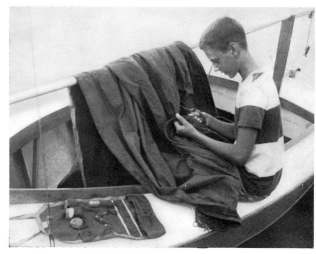

Keep your sails in good repair. Minor damage to batten pockets, servings, etc., can be easily and profitably repaired with the aid of a sail repair kit.

A schooner dries her sails by letting them hang loosely with booms in their boom-crotches. Don't attempt this if there is a strong current or in anything but very light airs.

Keep wet or damp sails out in the sun and air until you are able to dry them thoroughly rather than in a sailbag or under sailcovers.

CARE OF THE BOAT

Small centerboard boats can easily be beached for cleaning and painting. Be sure centerboard is pulled up and remove rudder if it extends below the keel. Where there is a tide bring the boat in at high water and pull her up as far as she will go on the evenest portion of beach.

Use a scraper or putty knife to remove barnacles and get right after the job while the bottom is still wet from the receding tide. They come off much easier while wet.

A stiff scrubbing brush is the best thing for use on marine grass, scum, etc. after you have scraped off all the barnacles. Keep the brush good and wet.

Wash down topsides, etc., with fresh water and washing powder on a soft scrubbing brush and rinse with clean water and a sponge.

Paint and varnish should be applied carefully. Be sure the surface has been washed down with fresh water and has been sandpapered to remove all loose material. Avoid damp, humid days and don't varnish in the heat of the midday sun or on a wet surface.

Grass, slime, and other marine growths can be quickly cleaned off small boats by turning them on their sides in shallow water.

Keel boats usually cannot be beached like centerboard boats but can be tied alongside a dock at high water and allowed to come to rest on their keels as the tide recedes. If you do this, be sure you know just how and where the keel will come to rest. Note the halliard taken out from the masthead to aid in keeping the boat upright.

MAKING FAST TO A CLEAT

Handling your boat may involve your first experience in making a line fast to a cleat. Learn to do it correctly.

line properly fastened to a cleat. First, a turn around the bottom, then a figure eight around the ends, and finally a couple of more turns around the bottom.

Don't make fast like this. A lot of figure eight turns with no final turn around the bottom can let go completely on the slightest provocation.

half-hitch like this should never be used in making sheets fast and avoided possible on halliards. It holds wonderfully but is likely to jam, especially if the line gets wet.

Jam cleats like this are often used for sheets or centerboard pennants but not for halliards. A single round turn makes this cleat hold.

KNOTS

Two or three simple knots are sufficient for all ordinary circumstances.
Learn to tie them correctly and the proper uses for each.

The Square Knot
The square knot is used for tying together the ends of two lines of similar size.

Begin the square-knot by twisting the two ends together. Then turn one end over alongside itself and pass the other end *over* each part — not over one and under the other. Getting the free end *over* both parts is the secret of a correct square knot.

Then twist the free ends together . . . and pull the knot tight.

KNOTS

The Bowline

The bowline is used for tying a loop in the end of a line. It is the best knot for tying a line to an anchor, tying a tow-line around a mast, etc. It will not slip or jam.

Begin the bowline by putting a loop in the standing part of the rope and passing the end up through this loop.

Then pass the end around the standing part, and down into the loop again.

Pull all four parts tight and the bowline is made.

From beneath the bowline will look like this.

KNOTS

The Clove-Hitch

The clove-hitch is most useful in tying to a post or stanchion.

Drop a turn over the post with the end over the standing part.

Then drop another turn over the post with the standing part underneath again and leading out in the opposite direction from the end.

Pull both ends tight and the clove-hitch is completed.

A false clove-hitch resulting from flipping the second turn the wrong way.

USING THE KNOTS

A granny knot which will not hold. It started out to be a square knot but the free end went *over* only one part.

This is a square-knot but it will not hold because there is too great a difference in the sizes of the two lines.

Use two bowlines like this to fasten together two lines of such dissimilar sizes.

HOW THE PICTURES WERE MADE

When Rufus Smith first spoke to me of his idea of doing an all picture book on sailing, my first thoughts were, naturally enough, of equipment. Fortunately, I had a plentiful assortment of cameras and lenses from which to choose. Thus, before work actually started I felt competent to meet any situation which might arise on the water. But soon after we started I found that no camera made could overcome our greatest problem. And that problem haunted us with the persistence of our own shadow. It cost us more in time, patience and confidence than anything else. We could do nothing about it and had to take it as it came. It was lack of wind. No camera could ever stir up a breeze, and without a breeze we could take no sailing pictures. We truly spent almost half our time waiting for sufficient wind to give the boat steerage way.

However, once a breeze did come in, Mr. Smith, like a Hollywood director, would shout his orders through a megaphone from the deck of his cruiser "Cough Drop" and I would prepare for action. Our day's work was well laid out in advance and we knew exactly what we wanted. Mr. Smith had to plan work in advance so that sequence pictures could be taken and no time lost in deliberation. Consequently the photographic problem was easier. If we had photographed haphazardly, I am sure that the book would have taken years instead of the two and a half months it did take us for the outdoor work.

The first camera I used was a 4x5 Speed Graphic with a 13.5 cm f/4.5 Zeiss Tessar lens. I thought we could use that for practically all the pictures, but found that because of the short focal length of the lens the image of the boat was often too small. Also it was difficult to get an accurate and quick focus when the boat was close to us and moving fast. Consequently it was advantageous to change over to a 4x5 Series D Graflex with a 7" f/4.5 Zeiss Tessar. This greatly facilitated following the action of the boat and maintaining focus at all times. Many of the pictures called for almost split second timing and for this the reflex camera was indispensable. The Graflex is pleasantly heavy and solid, which I found a big help on a bobbing boat at anchor as we were on the "Cough Drop." In spite of the seeming ponderousness of this camera I found it easy to handle and sequence pictures could be taken with surprising speed.

Being out on the water and having a maximum of light, exposures could be fast. Rather than clicking the shutter at extreme high speeds, I preferred to stop down the diaphragm to f/16. and expose at approximately 1/100th of a second, which stopped all necessary action. A Model D Leica with a 50 mm f/2. Sunmar lens was a big help in some closeup pictures.

The choice of film was interesting. I wanted a fairly fast film so I could close down the diaphragm for depth of focus. The very fast panchromatic films are rather grainy and their truer color rendition unimportant for this type of work. The final choice was Verichrome, an orthochromatic film which gave good rendition, medium speed and no grain to speak of when it was correctly developed. For the Leica, Panatomic film was used exclusively. Since several dozen pictures would be taken on a good day, film packs were used for convenience rather than cut film.

The pictures of the knots were all taken indoors with a 5x7 Ansco view camera, equipped with a 12″ f/6.8 Goerz Dagor lens. The problem was to get enough modelling on the crossovers of the line so that the eye could easily see which part was on top. The lights were placed with this in mind and the film (Eastman Super Sensitive Panchromatic) was overdeveloped to increase contrast.

In all, over five hundred pictures were taken of the Senior Knockabout, and from them Mr. Smith had the unenviable task of selecting the correct ones for the book. However, the really remarkable thing about the five hundred pictures is that each and every one of them was staged and rehearsed as carefully as a Broadway show.

WALTER CIVARDI

PHOTO CREDITS:

In addition to the photographs taken by Walter Civardi, the following are credited with the photographs on pages indicated:

M. Rosenfeld—pages 18, 19, 25, 27 (lower), 35, 43, 48 (lower), 52, 65 (lower), 66, 69 (lower), 71 (lower), 74, 81, 83 (lower), 88 (lower).

Chester Rogers—pages 2, 30, 65 (upper), 67, 84 (lower).

H. Devereux—pages 57, 69 (upper), 85.

H. H. Harris, Gen'l. Alloys Corp.—page 38.

John Kabel—page 15.